W9-BSG-901

ROBLOX

WHERE'S THE NOOB?

Written by Craig Jelley
Designed by John Stuckey and Maddox Philpot
Illustrations by Adam Doyle
Special thanks to the entire Roblox team

HARPER FESTIVAL
An Imprint of HarperCollinsPublishers

© 2019 Roblox Corporation.
"Roblox," the Roblox logo, and "Powering Imagination" are among the Roblox
registered and unregistered trademarks in the U.S. and other countries.

All rights reserved. Printed in Italy.
No part of this book may be used or reproduced in any manner whatsoever without
written permission except in the case of brief quotations embodied in critical articles and
reviews. For information address HarperCollins Children's Books, a division of HarperCollins
Publishers, 195 Broadway, New York, NY 10007.

ISBN 978-0-06-295018-5
❖
19 20 21 22 23 RTLO 10 9 8 7 6 5 4 3 2
First US Edition

Original English language edition first published in 2019 by Egmont UK Limited, The Yellow
Building, 1 Nicholas Road, London W11 4AN, United Kingdom.

Stay safe online. Any website addresses listed in this book are correct at the time of going to
print. However, HarperCollins is not responsible for content hosted by third parties. Please be
aware that online content can be subject to change and websites can contain content that is
unsuitable for children. We advise that all children are supervised when using the internet.

NOOB ON THE LOOSE

There's panic at Roblox HQ! A force of nature is creating a disturbance in several of the most popular games on the platform. It appears that something – no, someone – is hopping between the games and causing chaos!

THE NOOB

The Noob's a good guy – all he wants to do is play awesome games with his friends! But trouble has a way of following him around wherever he goes. Can you keep his bad luck from messing up the whole Roblox universe?

Builderman quickly assembles his most trusted friends, the Roblox Icons, to find The Noob and stop the havoc.

BUILDERMAN

He's the fearless leader of the Roblox team and one of the founding members of the platform. Everything he has worked so hard to create is in jeopardy. If anyone can find The Noob and get to the root of the problem, it's this guy!

EZEBEL: THE PIRATE QUEEN

Brave and fearless, Ezebel takes the lead on any adventure, whether on land, sea, or an online platform growing at an exponential rate. She's also used to working with a motley crew of oddballs, which will serve her well on this quest.

MR. BLING BLING

His charming smile and trustworthiness can open doors to all corners of Robloxia, making him a valuable asset. And if his smile doesn't work, then his endless riches may be able to grease the gears.

MR. ROBOT

Just as likely to be causing chaos himself, Mr. Robot will be invaluable to the team in deciphering how The Noob's chaos will unravel. Let's hope he doesn't go haywire in the process too.

REDCLIFF ELITE COMMANDER

A shining paragon of hope and valor, Redcliff Elite Commander is an indispensable hero to have at your side in a situation like this. He's fought for millennia to save Roblox from the Korbloxian menace, so this should be a piece of cake.

KORBLOX GENERAL

Some things are bigger than a war as old as time, so the Korblox General has halted his military campaign against Redcliff until order has been restored across Robloxia. Be sure to keep an eye on him, though.

Can you find every Roblox Icon in each game that The Noob visits?

GAMES PAGE

Unrest has been reported in the following games. You can visit them in order, or jump to your favorite game to try and put a stop to The Noob's pandemonium.

BUSTING OUT

Jailbreak by Badimo

OUT OF THE FRYING PAN

Roblox Deathrun by Team Deathrun

SAVING THE DAY

Heroes of Robloxia by Team Super

MAYHEM IN BLOXBURG

Welcome to Bloxburg by Coeptus

CLONE CONFUSION

Clone Tycoon 2 by Ultraw

DISASTER ZONE

Natural Disaster Survival by Stickmasterluke

PLAYGROUND PANIC

MeepCity by Alexnewtron

RISING TIDE

Flood Escape 2 by Crazyblox Games

ENCHANTMENT 101

Royale High by callmehbob

FRANTIC FUN FAIR

Theme Park Tycoon 2 by Den_S

HAVOC AT HIGHSCHOOL

Robloxian Highschool by RedManta

ZOMBIEPOCALYPSE

Zombie Rush by Beacon Studio

PIZZA PANDEMONIUM

Work at a Pizza Place by Dued1

HIDE AND SEEK HIJINKS

Hide and Seek Extreme by Tim7775

CATWALK CHAOS

Fashion Famous by PixelatedCandy

BUSTING OUT

Builderman has followed The Noob's trail of mayhem to Badimo's Jailbreak, where a riot has erupted. Can you spot The Noob and the rest of the Roblox Icons hiding in this chaotic prison scene?

Jailbreak

Badimo

OUT OF THE FRYING PAN

And into a fiery lava level! The Noob has joined the courageous runners in Roblox Deathrun. Can you spot him, Builderman, and the rest of the Roblox Icons before they're overwhelmed?

Roblox Deathrun

Team Deathrun

SAVING THE DAY

Swooping in to Heroes of Robloxia, The Noob finds himself caught between the brave superheroes and a band of thieves. Will he join the fight for justice or cower in a corner until the day is saved?

Heroes of Robloxia

Team Super

MAYHEM IN BLOXBURG

The citizens of Bloxburg are busy keeping the city running and building their dream houses. But The Noob can't be far, as chaos has descended on the town. Help return order to Bloxburg by finding the dastardly Robloxian.

Welcome to Bloxburg

Coeptus

CLONE CONFUSION

One Noob can be trouble, but give him a duplicating machine and there's no telling what he can do! Help the team find The Noob before he accidentally makes an army of replicant troublemakers.

Clone Tycoon 2

Ultraw

DISASTER ZONE

The Noob is blending in nicely with Natural Disaster Survival's disorder. This may be Builderman's toughest test yet! See if you can find all the characters while dodging the danger of the disaster-strewn island.

Natural Disaster Survival

Stickmasterluke

PLAYGROUND PANIC

Where better to hide than one of Roblox's most popular games? The Noob is somewhere among the hundreds of visitors to MeepCity, but with so much to do, will Builderman and his crew be able to focus on capturing him?

PET SHOP

ADOPT A MEEP

TOYS

MeepCity

Alexnewtron

RISING TIDE

As if the search for The Noob wasn't hard enough, Builderman must now contend with a catastrophic flood. Can you find the access panels that will grant dozens of Robloxians safe passage to the castle's high ground?

Flood Escape 2

Crazyblox Games

ENCHANTMENT 101

Normal methods have failed up to this point, so the Roblox Icons visit Royale High for some magical assistance in their quest to capture The Noob. Little do they know he is already among them, hiding in plain sight!

Royale High

callmehbob

FRANTIC FUN FAIR

The Noob has eluded Builderman's grasp once more and landed in Theme Park Tycoon 2, where screams can be heard for miles around. It's probably just the awesome rides, but you'd better help find him just in case!

Theme Park Tycoon 2

Den_S

HAVOC AT HIGHSCHOOL

The education bug seems to have bitten The Noob, so he's gone back to Robloxian Highschool. Builderman's intel has led him down to the school's sports field. Can you find The Noob and all the other Roblox Icons?

Robloxian Highschool

RedManta

ZOMBIEPOCALYPSE

Builderman and the gang have found themselves in Zombie Rush and they're no longer doing the chasing! Can they escape the flesh-hungry hordes and locate The Noob at the same time?

Zombie Rush

Beacon Studio

PIZZA PANDEMONIUM

Tracking down The Noob has made the team super hungry, so they pop into Work at a Pizza Place's Builder Brothers Pizza for some rest and refreshments. But what's this? Turmoil in the kitchen? Looks like The Noob is up to no good!

Top Collector

Builder Brothers PIZZA

STAR

Builder Brothers PIZZA

Work at a Pizza Place

Dued1

HIDE AND SEEK HIJINKS

The games on Roblox are larger-than-life – none more so than Hide and Seek Extreme, the next stop on Builderman's wild Noob chase. Can you spot the elusive Noob in this oversized attic scene?

Hide and Seek Extreme

Tim7775

CATWALK CHAOS

Roblox fashionistas are choosing outfits, donning wings, and competing to become truly Fashion Famous. Little do they know, The Noob is about to give everyone zero stars so he can claim the crown for himself. Can you find him and all the stylish Roblox Icons?

Fashion Famous

PixelatedCandy

MORE THINGS TO FIND

You're coming to the end of your hectic tour of the Roblox universe, with The Noob safely under the watch of Builderman and the Roblox Icons. But how closely were you paying attention? Retrace your way through the games to see if you can find these items hidden in each scene.

BUSTING OUT
- ☐ 1 police chopper
- ☐ 2 escape ladders
- ☐ 2 sleeping guards
- ☐ 3 blue keycards
- ☐ 4 riot officers

OUT OF THE FRYING PAN
- ☐ 2 diamonds
- ☐ 2 firework spots
- ☐ 3 green trap buttons
- ☐ 4 sparkle-trailed runners
- ☐ 5 golden coins

SAVING THE DAY
- ☐ Dynamo
- ☐ Tessla
- ☐ Captain Roblox
- ☐ Kinetic
- ☐ Overdrive

MAYHEM IN BLOXBURG

- ☐ 1 pizza delivery driver
- ☐ 2 graffiti cleaners
- ☐ 3 fishermen
- ☐ 4 lumberjacks
- ☐ 5 broken-down motorbikes

CLONE CONFUSION

- ☐ 1 giant woman with glasses
- ☐ 2 penguin pets
- ☐ 3 transport ships
- ☐ 4 mech clones
- ☐ 5 Noob clones (no face)

DISASTER ZONE

- ☐ 1 golden compass
- ☐ 2 falling meteors
- ☐ 3 diggers
- ☐ 4 green balloons
- ☐ 5 flaming barrels

PLAYGROUND PANIC

- ☐ The MeepCity Fisherman
- ☐ 2 blue and yellow racecars
- ☐ 3 Starball stars
- ☐ 4 triple-scoop ice creams
- ☐ 5 red Meeps

RISING TIDE

- ☐ 1 green access panel
- ☐ 2 Mini Crazy Buddies
- ☐ 3 sparkly-trailed players
- ☐ 4 yellow cursors
- ☐ 5 rainbow tanks

ENCHANTMENT 101

- ☐ 1 mermaid textbook
- ☐ 2 heart-winged students
- ☐ 3 A-star grades
- ☐ 4 cupcakes
- ☐ 5 orange potions

FRANTIC FUN FAIR

- ☐ 1 umbrella seating area
- ☐ 2 rollercoaster cars
- ☐ 3 burger stands
- ☐ 4 cacti
- ☐ 5 dino hats

HAVOC AT HIGHSCHOOL

- ☐ 1 giant blimp
- ☐ 2 skydivers
- ☐ 3 science experiments
- ☐ 4 footballs
- ☐ 5 hoverboarders

ZOMBIEPOCALYPSE

- ☐ 1 giant red gummy bear
- ☐ 2 diamond brutes
- ☐ 3 phantoms
- ☐ 4 discarded laser guns
- ☐ 5 gold skeletons

PIZZA PANDEMONIUM

- ☐ 1 Builder Brothers supply truck
- ☐ 2 chefs with fire extinguishers
- ☐ 3 full pepperoni pizzas
- ☐ 4 delivery scooters
- ☐ 5 cockroaches

HIDE AND SEEK HIJINKS

- ☐ 1 boombox
- ☐ 2 Tee Vee accessories
- ☐ 3 tripod cameras
- ☐ 4 glue bottles
- ☐ 5 coins

CATWALK CHAOS

- ☐ 1 elephant in a skirt
- ☐ 2 mermaid-tailed characters
- ☐ 3 orange-winged characters
- ☐ 4 llama pets
- ☐ 5 crowns

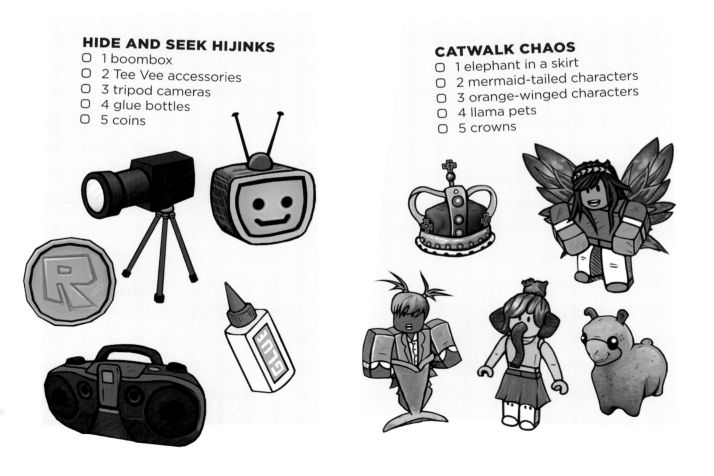

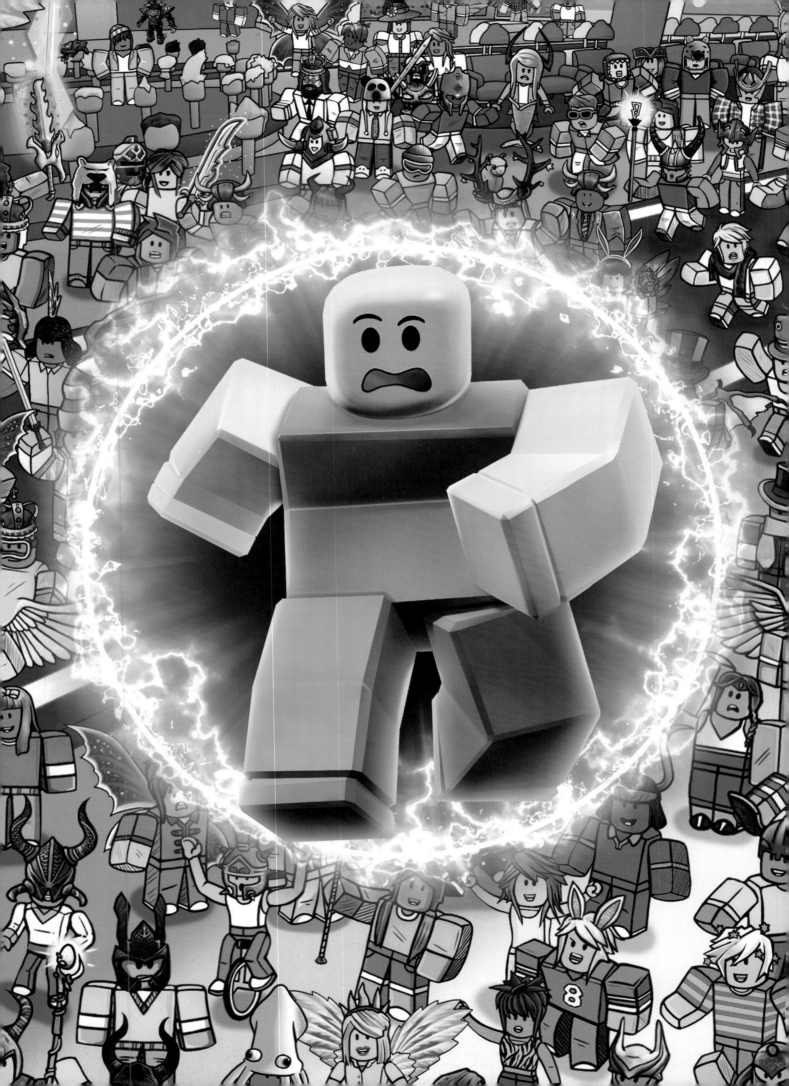